The BILL of RIGHTS

Congrefs OF THE United States

begun and held at the City of New-York, on
Wednesday the fourth of March, one thousand seven hundred and eighty nine

THE Conventions of a number of the States, having at the time of their adopting the Constitution, expressed a desire, in order to prevent misconstruction or abuse of its powers, that further declaratory and restrictive clauses should be added: And as extending the ground of public confidence in the Government, will best ensure the beneficent ends of its institution.

RESOLVED by the Senate and House of Representatives of the United States of America, in Congress assembled, two thirds of both Houses concurring, that the following Articles be proposed to the Legislatures of the several States, as amendments to the Constitution of the United States, all, or any of which Articles, when ratified by three fourths of the said Legislatures, to be valid to all intents and purposes, as part of the said Constitution; viz.

ARTICLES in addition to, and Amendment of the Constitution of the United States of America, proposed by Congress, and ratified by the Legislatures of the several States, pursuant to the fifth Article of the original Constitution.

Article the first... After the first enumeration required by the first Article of the Constitution, there shall be one Representative for every thirty thousand, until the number shall amount to one hundred, after which the proportion shall be so regulated by Congress, that there shall be not less than one hundred Representatives, nor less than one Representative for every forty thousand persons, until the number of Representatives shall amount to two hundred, after which the proportion shall be so regulated by Congress, that there shall not be less than two hundred Representatives, nor more than one Representative for every fifty thousand persons.

Article the second... No law, varying the compensation for the services of the Senators and Representatives, shall take effect, until an election of Representatives shall have intervened.

Article the third... Congress shall make no law respecting an establishment of religion, or prohibiting the free exercise thereof; or abridging the freedom of speech, or of the press; or the right of the people peaceably to assemble, and to petition the Government for a redress of grievances.

Article the fourth... A well regulated militia, being necessary to the security of a free State, the right of the people to keep and bear arms, shall not be infringed.

Article the fifth... No soldier shall, in time of peace be quartered in any house, without the consent of the owner, nor in time of war, but in a manner to be prescribed by law.

Article the sixth... The right of the people to be secure in their persons, houses, papers, and effects, against unreasonable searches and seizures, shall not be violated, and no Warrants shall issue, but upon probable cause, supported by oath or affirmation, and particularly describing the place to be searched, and the persons or things to be seized.

Article the seventh... No person shall be held to answer for a capital, or otherwise infamous crime, unless on a presentment or indictment of a Grand Jury, except in cases arising in the land or naval forces, or in the Militia, when in actual service in time of War or public danger; nor shall any person be subject for the same offence to be twice put in jeopardy of life or limb; nor shall be compelled in any criminal case to be a witness against himself, nor be deprived of life, liberty, or property, without due process of law; nor shall private property be taken for public use, without just compensation.

Article the eighth... In all criminal prosecutions, the accused shall enjoy the right to a speedy and public trial, by an impartial jury of the State and district wherein the crime shall have been committed, which district shall have been previously ascertained by law, and to be informed of the nature and cause of the accusation; to be confronted with the witnesses against him; to have compulsory process for obtaining witnesses in his favor, and to have the assistance of Counsel for his defence.

Article the ninth... In suits at common law, where the value in controversy shall exceed twenty dollars, the right of trial by jury shall be preserved, and no fact tried by a jury, shall be otherwise re-examined in any Court of the United States, than according to the rules of the common law.

Article the tenth... Excessive bail shall not be required, nor excessive fines imposed, nor cruel and unusual punishments inflicted.

Article the eleventh... The enumeration in the Constitution, of certain rights, shall not be construed to deny or disparage others retained by the people.

Article the twelfth... The powers not delegated to the United States by the Constitution, nor prohibited by it to the States, are reserved to the States respectively, or to the people.

ATTEST,

Frederick Augustus Muhlenberg, Speaker of the House of Representatives

John Adams, Vice President of the United States, and President of the Senate

John Beckley, Clerk of the House of Representatives.
Sam. A. Otis, Secretary of the Senate.

documents of
DEMOCRACY

The
BILL
of **RIGHTS**

by stephen krensky

MARSHALL CAVENDISH BENCHMARK
NEW YORK

With thanks to Catherine McGlone,
a lawyer with a special interest in constitutional law and American history,
for her legal eagle eye in perusing the manuscript.

Other Marshall Cavendish Offices:
Marshall Cavendish International (Asia) Private Limited, 1 New Industrial Road, Singapore 536196
• Marshall Cavendish International (Thailand) Co Ltd. 253 Asoke, 12th Flr, Sukhumvit 21 Road,
Klongtoey Nua, Wattana, Bangkok 10110, Thailand • Marshall Cavendish (Malaysia) Sdn Bhd, Times
Subang, Lot 46, Subang Hi-Tech Industrial Park, Batu Tiga, 40000 Shah Alam, Selangor Darul
Ehsan, Malaysia

Marshall Cavendish is a trademark of Times Publishing Limited
All websites were available and accurate when this book was sent to press.

LIBRARY OF CONGRESS CATALOGING-IN-PUBLICATION DATA
Krensky, Stephen. The Bill of Rights / Stephen Krensky. p. cm. — (Documents of democracy)
Includes bibliographical references and index. Summary: "An analysis of the U.S. Bill of Rights,
with information on how it was created and how it has evolved, with examples of major Supreme
Court decisions related to it"—Provided by publisher. ISBN 978-0-7614-4912-6 — ISBN 978-
1-60870-669-3 (ebook) 1. United States. Constitution. 1st-10th Amendments—History. 2. Civil
rights—United States—History. I. Title. KF4749.K746 2012 342.7308'5—dc22 2010042489

Editor: Joyce Stanton   Art Director: Anahid Hamparian
Publisher: Michelle Bisson   Series Designer: Michael Nelson

Photo research by Linda Sykes Picture Research, Inc., Hilton Head, SC
The photographs in this book are used by permission and through the courtesy of: Shutterstock: cover;
iStockphoto: 1; The Granger Collection: 2, 8, 11, 15, 18, 22, 23, 26, 32, 50, 63; Virginia Historical
Society: 6; ©Ocean/Corbis: 28; Collection of the New-York Historical Society/The Bridgeman Art
Library: 46; Bettmann/Corbis: 53; Jose Luis Magana/AP Images: 57; Seattle History Museum: 58;
©Corbis: 59.

Printed in Malaysia (T)
135642

Half-title page: The Bill of Rights
**Title page: The original document containing the first ten amendments to the Constitution
did not include the title by which we know the Bill of Rights today.**

Contents

Promises *to* Keep

The stakes were high. If nothing else, the 168 delegates meeting in Richmond, Virginia, in early June 1788 could agree on that. Their purpose, after all, was clear and far-reaching—to decide whether the state of Virginia should ratify the Constitution of the United States.

The Federalists, as those favoring ratification were known, believed that a strong national government was essential for the healthy survival of the thirteen former British colonies. They were led by thirty-seven-year-old James Madison, which was hardly a surprise. It was Madison who had written much of the Constitution as a delegate to the Constitutional Convention in Philadelphia the previous summer.

The Anti-Federalists, including such patriots as Virginia's George Mason and Patrick Henry, opposed ratifying the Constitution. Henry feared that the new government would be too powerful, and that over time it would dictate unacceptable directives to the states.

Above: James Madison addresses the Constitutional Convention in this 1830 painting by George Catlin.

Mason's objection was a bit different. Where in this document, he wondered, were the fundamental liberties of the people protected? He was thinking of the certain "unalienable rights" with which people were "endowed by their Creator." These rights cited in the Declaration of Independence were part of a higher law, one that stood above laws created by any government. Unless they were clearly protected, Mason could not endorse the new framework for government.

On June 4, the third day of the meeting, Mason made his feelings clearly known. "Is it to be supposed that one National Government will suit so extensive a country, embracing so many climates, and containing inhabitants so very different in manners, habits, and customs?" he asked. "It is ascertained by history, that there never was a Government, over a very extensive country, without destroying the liberties of the people."

Perhaps the promise of a bill of rights, introduced as amendments to the Constitution, would reassure the doubters. It would address both Mason's and Henry's concerns. A bill of rights would put a check on the strong national government established by the Constitution and would clearly spell out the personal liberties that needed protecting. Such a bill had been promised to delegates in several of the other states that had debated ratification. Would a similar promise be enough to win over the reluctant Virginia delegates? Hanging on that question was the future of the so-called United States of America.

deny or disparage others retained by the people

The inauguration of President George Washington in April 1789 on the balcony of New York's Federal Hall. Washington, D.C., had not yet been built.

Chapter One

A Question *of* Rights

FOR THE CITIZENS OF THE NEW UNITED States, the spring of 1789 was well worth noting. On April 30, George Washington of Virginia, the former commander in chief of the Continental army, was inaugurated as the country's first president. This was a big moment. People were used to Washington leading the country in a time of war, but that time had passed. The American Revolution was over, and peace had been established. Now the thirteen states had created a new government based on a new document—the Constitution. It provided for three separate branches of government: the executive, the legislative, and the judicial. As president, George Washington was head of the executive branch. The legislative branch was composed of a two-part Congress: the House of Representatives and the Senate. The Supreme Court, having final authority over a system of lower courts, made up the judicial branch.

Washington's inauguration was just the latest in a series of extraordinary political changes to sweep the country. Those changes had begun thirteen years earlier, with the publication of the Declaration of Independence. That momentous event had thrust the colonies into five years of war with Great Britain. In 1783, the Treaty of Paris had made the separation from Britain official. The thirteen colonies were finally free.

But independence, while settling a great many issues, also raised new questions. How should the thirteen states go forward? Should they stick together in one group? Or should they split along geographic lines? And if they did split, how many "pieces" would make sense?

Up to this point, the country had been operating under the guidelines of the Articles of Confederation, a set of rules drawn up during the Revolution by the Second Continental Congress and agreed upon by the states. But the Articles had a number of limitations. They gave each state a single vote in Congress, regardless of the state's size and population. Also, any one state could veto a proposed piece of legislation, even if the other twelve were in complete agreement. The biggest problem, however, was that the Articles did not give Congress the power to raise money for national purposes. In order to get anything done, it had to rely completely on voluntary contributions from the states. And such contributions were hard to get.

Hoping to improve the situation, delegates gathered in Philadelphia in the spring of 1787. Representatives from every state except Rhode Island attended the convention. (Leaders in Rhode Island steadfastly opposed any changes to the Articles that would affect the state's ability to govern itself.) Initially, many delegates thought that simply revising the Articles of Confederation was the best course. But the momentum soon shifted toward creating a whole new framework of government, and the Constitution was born.

This cartoon shows the steps leading from the Articles of Confederation to the Constitution.

REACHING INTO THE PAST

From the beginning of the Constitutional Convention, some delegates wanted to include a bill of rights. Such rights had a long and proud place in English law. Even though the delegates were gathering to create a new form of government, English law (without the offending monarchy) was still the foundation of their thinking.

The "rights of Englishmen," as they were known, had evolved over the course of many centuries. They had come about as a result of the gradual chipping away of the power of the monarch. The power struggle was at first between the king and his nobles and later between the king and the members of Parliament. The first document attesting to these disputes was the Magna Carta, an agreement forced upon King John I in 1215 by his rebellious barons. The Magna Carta declared that a king's actions were not above the law but were instead subject to the law. The barons had reached this conclusion after King John had lost a great many battles and then arrogantly raised taxes to help pay for them. The Magna Carta protected the rights of the powerful nobles of its time. It would be revised often and would eventually come to be thought of as the basis of English democracy.

Nearly five hundred years after King John signed the Magna Carta, the actions of another difficult king prompted further advances in the rights of Englishmen. King James II was a devout Catholic in an England that had been Protestant for more than a hundred years. Moreover, he believed in the absolute power of the monarchy. In 1688, in what became known as the Glorious Revolution, he was forced to abdicate and leave the country. Parliament asked his Protestant son-in-law, William of Orange, to come over from the Netherlands to replace him. It was at this time that Parliament seized the opportunity to restrain the power of the monarchy and institutionalize some personal liberties. The English Bill of Rights was presented to the new king when he ascended the throne. It banned the monarch from meddling with existing laws, acting as a judge in court cases, and raising taxes without Parliament's consent. It also prohibited the government from keeping a standing army among the population during peacetime unless approved by Parliament. Another provision allowed Protestants to keep arms for their own defense, and there was a general allowance for freedom of speech.

THE RIGHTS OF COLONISTS

As the eighteenth century unfolded, the movement to limit the power of the monarch and protect individual liberties gained momentum. In the 1760s, colonial Americans objected when they were treated unfairly by their mother country. "No taxation without representation!" was their most famous cry. Unfortunately, Great Britain was too busy trying to raise money to listen to their protests.

As the American colonists grew angrier and angrier, they formalized the rights they believed they were entitled to. New Hampshire and South Carolina drew up constitutions in early 1776. Other states soon followed. The most notable of these early documents was the Virginia Constitution, written just weeks before the publication of the Declaration of Independence.

The main author of Virginia's constitution was George Mason. He was fifty-one years old, married, and the father of nine children. He had first entered political life as a

THE VIRGINIA DECLARATION OF RIGHTS

The Virginia Declaration of Rights was written just a few weeks before the Declaration of Independence and was unanimously adopted on June 12, 1776. It enumerated many ideas that later were included in the Bill of Rights. It contained sixteen articles (shown on the next page) designed to outline both the responsibilities and the limits of government.

Among its now familiar concepts were the following ideas:

> that in all capital or criminal prosecutions a man hath a right to demand the cause and nature of his accusation, to be confronted with the accusers and witnesses, to call for evidence in his favor, and to a speedy trial by an impartial jury of twelve men of his vicinage, . . . that excessive bail ought not to be required, nor excessive fines imposed, nor cruel and unusual punishments inflicted . . . , that the freedom of the press is one of the great bulwarks of liberty and . . . that all men are equally entitled to the free exercise of religion.

THE VIRGINIA DECLARATION OF RIGHTS

A Declaration of Rights made by the Representatives of the Good People of Virginia, assembled in Full and Free Convention; which Rights do pertain to Them and their Posterity, as the Basis and Foundation of Government.

ARTICLE I.

THAT all Men are by Nature equally free and independent, and have certain inherent Rights, of which, when they enter into a State of Society, they cannot, by any Compact, deprive or divest their Posterity; namely, the Enjoyment of Life and Liberty, with the Means of acquiring and possessing Property, and pursuing and obtaining Happiness and Safety.

ARTICLE II.

THAT all Power is vested in, and consequently derived from, the People; that Magistrates are their Trustees and Servants, and at all Times amenable to them.

ARTICLE III.

THAT Government is, or ought to be, instituted for the common Benefit, Protection, and Security, of the People, Nation, or Community; of all the various Modes and Forms of Government that is best, which is capable of producing the greatest Degree of Happiness and Safety, and is most effectually secured against the Danger of Mal-administration; and that, whenever any Government shall be found inadequate or contrary to these Purposes, a Majority of the Community hath an indubitable, unalienable, and indefeasible Right, to reform, alter, or abolish it, in such Manner as shall be judged most conducive to the public Weal.

ARTICLE IV.

THAT no Man, or Set of Men, are entitled to exclusive or seperate Emoluments or Priviliges from the Community, but in Consideration of public Service; which, not being descendible, neither ought the Offices of Magistrate, Legislator, or Judge, to be hereditary.

ARTICLE V.

THAT the legislative and executive Powers of the State should be seperate and distinct from the Judicative; and, that the Members of the two first may be restrained from Oppression, by feeling and participating in the Burthens of the People, they should, at fixed Periods, be reduced to a private Station, return into that Body from which they were originally taken, and the Vacancies be supplied by frequent, certain, and regular Elections, in which all, or any Part of the former Members, to be again eligible, or ineligible, as the Laws shall direct.

ARTICLE VI.

THAT Elections of Members to serve as Representatives of the People, in Assembly, ought to be free: and that all Men, having sufficient Evidence of permanent common Interest with, and Attachment to, the Community, have the Right of Suffrage, and cannot be taxed or deprived of their Property for public Uses without their own Consent or that of their Representatives so elected, nor bound by any Law to which they have not, in like Manner, assented, for the public Good.

ARTICLE VII.

THAT all Power of suspending Laws, or the Execution of Laws, by any Authority without Consent of the Representatives of the People, is injurious to their Rights, and ought not to be exercised.

ARTICLE VIII.

THAT in all capital or criminal Prosecutions a Man hath a Right to demand the Cause and Nature of his Accusation, to be confronted with the Accusers and Witnesses, to call for Evidence in his Favour, and to a speedy Trial by an impartial Jury of his Vicinage without whose unanimous Consent he cannot be found guilty, nor can he be compelled to give Evidence against himself; that no Man be deprived of his Liberty except by the Law of the Land, or the Judgement of his Peers.

ARTICLE IX.

THAT excessive Bail ought not to be required, nor excessive Fines imposed; nor cruel and unusual Punishments inflicted.

ARTICLE X.

THAT general Warrants, whereby any Officer or Messenger may be commanded to search suspected Places without Evidence of a Fact committed, or to seize any Person or Persons not named, or whose Offence is not particularly described and supported by Evidence, are grievous and oppressive, and ought not to be granted.

ARTICLE XI.

THAT in Controversies respecting Property, and in Suits between Man and Man, the ancient Trial by Jury is preferable to any other, and ought to be held sacred.

ARTICLE XII.

THAT the Freedom of the Press is one of the greatest Bulwarks of Liberty, and can never be restrained but by despotic Governments.

ARTICLE XIII.

THAT a well regulated Militia, composed of the Body of the People, trained to Arms, is the proper, natural, and safe Defense of a free State; that standing Armies, in Time of Peace, should be avoided, as dangerous to Liberty; and that, in all Cases, that the Military should be under strict Subordination to, and governed by, the Civil Power.

ARTICLE XIV.

THAT the People have a Right to uniform Government; and therefore, that no Government; seperate from, the Government of Virginia, ought to be erected or established within the Limits thereof.

ARTICLE XV.

THAT no free Government, or the Blessing of Liberty, can be preserved to any People but by a firm Adherence to Justice, Moderation, Temperance, Frugality, and Virtue, and by frequent Recurrence to fundamental Principles.

ARTICLE XVI.

THAT Religion, or the Duty which we owe to our Creator, and the Manner of discharging it, can be directed only by Reason and Conviction, not by Force or Violence; and therefore, all Men are equally entitled to the free exercise of Religion, according to the Dictates of Conscience; and that it is the mutual Duty of all to practice Christian Forbearance, Love, and Charity, towards each other.

Drawn originally by GEORGE MASON and adopted unanimously by the Convention of Delegates at the Capitol in Williamsburg on June 12, 1776.

member of Virginia's colonial legislature, the House of Burgesses, in 1759. By 1776, he was a delegate to the Virginia Convention, the political body that had taken the place of the House of Burgesses after the British governor dissolved it. Unlike his fellow delegates Thomas Jefferson and James Madison, Mason had not attended college. He had educated himself mostly by reading from his uncle's library of 1,500 books. The library must have been a good one, because Mason distinguished himself among his peers. He helped write the Virginia Constitution and was the primary author of the Virginia Declaration of Rights, both of which were composed in the spring of 1776. Parts of these documents found echoes in the Declaration of Independence that shortly followed.

THE CONSTITUTIONAL CONVENTION

In May 1787, Mason was one of the Virginia delegates to the Constitutional Convention in Philadelphia. Since many states besides Virginia had also enacted constitutions stipulating individual rights, he assumed that a national constitution would do the same. But he was mistaken.

The prime movers behind the U.S. Constitution were focused on creating a framework for running a national government. Individual rights and liberties certainly mattered to them, but it was more important to create a well-balanced, effective government in which power could be shared fairly and the threat of tyranny minimized. Delegates, for example, pondered long and hard on the makeup of the legislative branch. They finally decided on a bicameral (two-house) Congress, which would provide fair representation for both the large and small states. They also wrestled with determining which powers and responsibilities were truly national and which more properly belonged to the individual states.

They also had to deal with the thorny issue of slavery. Most delegates from the North were opposed to slavery, and many from the South were as well (even some of those who owned slaves). But slavery was integral to the economies of certain states, especially South Carolina and Georgia. Eliminating it was not feasible—if the ultimate goal was to keep all the states united.

To complicate things even more, some leaders at the convention believed that a dangerous precedent would be set by explicitly guaranteeing certain personal liberties in the Constitution. What if some rights were left out? Did that mean they weren't important? Or could it mean that any right not specifically cited would remain only at the discretion of the new federal government?

Roger Sherman of Connecticut maintained that a bill of rights was not needed because the states had covered such concerns for themselves. Moreover, the Constitution stated that whatever power was not expressly given to the federal government would be

John Hancock, one of the most prominent leaders of the American Revolution, as portrayed by John Singleton Copley in 1765

retained by the states. So unless the Constitution was expressly prohibiting certain rights—which it wasn't—there was no need for further action.

Not everyone was convinced by such arguments. Those who wanted a bill of rights and those who opposed the Constitution on other grounds joined forces to try to defeat passage of the Constitution. Mason himself announced during the final weeks of the convention that he would "sooner chop off his right hand than put it to the Constitution as it now stands."

Some of the delegates even called for a second convention to be held. This first one, they claimed, had so overstepped its original bounds that another was both necessary and proper. But the Constitution's supporters were wary of beginning again. They recognized that they would never get everyone to agree on everything, and they were reasonably pleased with the document they had. The new Constitution was a radical step forward in many ways, encompassing both old and new ideas. It might not be perfect, but it was perfect enough. These arguments convinced enough delegates to put their reservations aside.

On September 17, 1787, the delegates met for the last time to sign the Constitution.

THE NEXT STEP

The Federalists had succeeded in getting the Constitution adopted, but none of them were celebrating just yet. The debate was far from over. Nine of the thirteen states had to ratify the Constitution before it would become binding. Separate conventions would be held in each state to vote on the issue, and nobody was confident enough to predict the eventual outcome.

It took only a few days for the Constitution to be widely published in newspapers, and the varied reactions came swiftly. There were both the expected approvals from the backers of a strong federal government and the objections from those who feared concentrating so much power in a centralized command.

What was not so expected, however, was the continued outcry over the lack of protection for personal liberties.

The Federalists had maintained all along that individual states were already guaranteeing many rights. But even if this was true, the protected rights in each state were not identical, and no state's constitution had jurisdiction over the new national government. What would happen if the national government ignored one state's particular law? Even worse, what if the new government ignored a lot of them?

"I think liberty a thing of too much importance to be trusted on the ground of implication: it should rest on principles expressed in the clearest & most unequivocal manner."

—William Grayson, Virginia statesman

These concerns made many people nervous. Starting a new government was a real leap of faith. Many Americans wanted explicit safeguards to protect their most dearly held values. Maybe a bill of rights would be redundant—or maybe it wouldn't. Either way, it wouldn't hurt to have one. This view was sharply summed up by William Grayson of Virginia: "I think liberty a thing of too much importance to be trusted on the ground of implication: it should rest on principles expressed in the clearest & most unequivocal manner."

Still, the Federalists continued to insist that the Constitution be approved. Newspaper articles began to appear several times a week in favor of ratification. These articles, written anonymously under the name of "Publius," were composed mostly by Alexander Hamilton and James Madison (with a few coming from New Yorker John Jay). Between October 1787 and August 1788, eighty-five articles, soon to be known as the Federalist Papers, were published. They endeavored to review every word of the Constitution, explaining how and why it appeared as it did. They also sought to explain why certain things were excluded, such as a bill of rights.

Some states needed no further convincing. Delaware, Pennsylvania, and New Jersey all voted to ratify the Constitution in December 1787. Georgia and Connecticut followed early the next month. With five states on board, only four more were needed to put the Constitution into effect.

A SIGNIFICANT CONCESSION

Getting those four states would not be easy. The leaders in the first five states had been fairly confident that everything would work out. And they had voted accordingly. Leaders in the remaining states were not so trusting. As the debate over ratification continued, the question of including a bill of rights loomed front and center.

The issue first became critical in Massachusetts, an important state both economically and politically. When delegates met at the state convention in the early winter of 1788, the conflict over ratification was anything but settled. Notable figures including the governor were against ratification. Initially, they held a majority of the vote.

Hoping to achieve a compromise, John Hancock and Sam Adams, prominent patriots since before the Revolution, proposed that the Constitution be ratified on one condition—that a bill of rights in the form of amendments to the Constitution be promptly drawn

Along with John Hancock, Sam Adams (facing page) proposed that the Bill of Rights be added to the Constitution.

up once the new government was established. Under the circumstances, there was no way this agreement could be legally enforced. However, the delegates making this commitment, many of whom hoped to be part of the new national government, were taken at their word. The formal vote in Massachusetts came on February 6, 1788. It was close—187 to 168 voted in favor of ratification. Without the promise of a future bill of rights, the vote likely would have gone the other way.

Although Massachusetts was now safely in the Federalist column, the recommendation of a bill of rights was a significant victory for the Anti-Federalists. Six of the remaining states would later append similar recommendations.

When the New Hampshire convention was adjourned by Federalists who sensed imminent defeat and when Rhode Island on March 24 turned down the Constitution in a popular referendum by an overwhelming vote of 10 to 1, Federalist leaders were apprehensive. Looking ahead to the Maryland convention, Madison wrote of his concerns to Washington, but in the end had little reason to worry. The final vote on April 28 was 63 for, 11 against. Maryland's citizens were jubilant. In Baltimore, a huge parade celebrating the Federalist victory rolled through the streets.

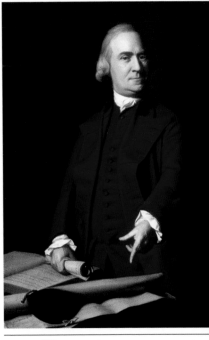

On July 2, 1788, the Confederation Congress, meeting in New York, received word that a reconvened New Hampshire ratifying convention had approved the Constitution. With South Carolina's acceptance of the Constitution in May, New Hampshire thus became the ninth state to ratify. The Congress appointed a committee "for putting the said Constitution into operation."

In the next two months, thanks largely to the efforts of Madison and Hamilton in their own states, Virginia and New York both ratified while adding their own amendments. (North Carolina and Rhode Island would ratify only after the new government was operating the next year.) The margin for the Federalists in both Virginia and New York was extremely close. Hamilton figured that the majority of the people in New York actually opposed the Constitution, and it is probable that a majority of people in the entire country opposed it. Only the promise of amendments had ensured a Federalist victory.

In the spring of 1789, shortly after the opening of the first session of Congress, a bill of rights was presented in the House of Representatives. James Madison, now a congressman from Virginia, introduced the subject on May 4. The other members of the House did not seem in any particular hurry to act, but Madison prodded them repeatedly. "It cannot be a secret to the gentlemen in this House," he told his colleagues on June 8, "that, notwithstanding the ratification of this system of Government . . . there is still a great number of our constituents who are dissatisfied with it. . . . We ought not to disregard their inclination but . . . conform to their wishes and expressly declare the great rights of Mankind."

> *"It cannot be a secret to the gentlemen in this House that . . . there is still a great number of our constituents who are dissatisfied. . . . We ought not to disregard their inclination but . . . conform to their wishes and expressly declare the great rights of Mankind."*
>
> *—James Madison, addressing the first Congress*

As different proposals were evaluated, dozens of amendments were circulated. Eventually, seventeen amendments surfaced with the strongest support. In August, they were sent to the Senate for consideration. The Senate decided that seventeen was too many to approve and proceeded to cut down the list.

Representatives from the House and Senate then met to iron out their differences. They agreed on twelve amendments, and these were passed on September 25, 1789. A week later, on October 2, President Washington officially sent them to the states for ratification.

Although the amendments were thought of as a group, each one had to be accepted or rejected on its own. Two did not receive the necessary three-fourths approval to become law, mainly because they were viewed as not relating to individual liberties and therefore not crucial to the moment. One of these amendments called for representation in the House to be maintained at a rate of one representative for every 30,000 people. The other concerned pay raises for the members of Congress and stipulated that any raises they voted for themselves could take effect only after a congressional election had intervened. (This last one, which was under no time limit for ratification, would become part of the Constitution as the Twenty-seventh Amendment in 1992.)

By December 15, 1791, three-fourths of the states had ratified the ten amendments. At that time, the amendments were added to the Constitution and afterward became known collectively as the Bill of Rights.

PROHIBITION ESTABLISHED — 1920 BY CONSTITUTIONAL AMENDMENT

TIME LIMITS ON RATIFYING AMENDMENTS

Initially, there was no time limit on how long an amendment to the Constitution might wait for ratification by the states. In theory, an amendment might have a rush of early support, followed by decades of inactivity, and then either fast or slow progress

Above: The constitutional amendment establishing the prohibition on alcohol sales and transportation in the United States was probably the most unpopular amendment ever.

toward final acceptance. In practice, however, an amendment that lost early momentum tended to be doomed. Beginning with the Eighteenth Amendment in 1920 (which banned the manufacture, sale, and transportation of alcohol), Congress required that any new amendment be ratified within seven years. After that, the amendment would expire. Should there be interest in it again, the process would have to start over from the beginning in Congress.

This change did not affect any amendments that were still pending approval by the states, and there were several of those. As it happened, Massachusetts, Georgia, and Connecticut never initially approved the amendments that made up the Bill of Rights. Technically, they didn't have to, because once three-quarters of the states had done so, the rest were bound by the new amendments whether they acted or not. However, as a symbolic gesture, these three states did finally ratify the first ten amendments on their 150th anniversaries, in 1939.

We the People

Bill of Rights

Congress of the United States

begun and held at the City of New York, on

Wednesday the Fourth of March, one thousand seven hundred and eighty nine

THE

RESOLVED

ARTICLES

Article the first ....

Article the second ....

Article the third ....

Article the fourth ....

Article the fifth ....

Article the sixth ....

Article the seventh ....

Article the eighth ....

Article the ninth ....

Article the tenth ....

Article the eleventh ....

Article the twelfth ....

Frederick Augustus Muhlenberg, Speaker of the House of Representatives.

John Adams, Vice President of the United States, and

ATTEST.

John Beckley, Clerk of the House of Representatives.

Sam. A. Otis, Secretary of the Senate.

Chapter Two

"The Great Rights *of* Mankind"

THE MOST NOTABLE ASPECT OF THE
Bill of Rights was not that it was enacted, or that it was
enacted quickly, but that it was enacted with so little
opposition. At the Constitutional Convention, delegates had argued about every detail of the new plan
for government. How powerful should the president be?
What proportions of checks and balances would make
the three branches of government mesh properly? What
was the best and fairest way for the people to be represented in Congress?

Yet when it came to the Bill of Rights, no real
opposition appeared. Admittedly, the movement toward
acceptance was propelled by an ongoing fear that the
federal government might trample personal liberties
if left unchecked. Still, such unanimity of purpose was
extraordinary. Conservative or liberal, rich or poor, big
state or small state, everyone seemed to be in agreement

about the need for, as James Madison had earlier declared, a clear and unambiguous declaration of the "great rights of Mankind."

THE PREAMBLE TO THE BILL OF RIGHTS

In 1789, everything about the federal government was still so new that it was worth noting again. The preamble to the Bill of Rights summarized the steps that had led up to the first ten amendments to the Constitution. It referred to their passage in Congress and subsequent approval by three-quarters of the state legislatures. And in case there was any doubt about the reason for formalizing these rights, the preamble made it clear: "The Conventions of a number of the States, having at the time of their adopting the Constitution, expressed a desire, in order to prevent misconstruction or abuse of its powers, that further declaratory and restrictive clauses should be added: And as extending the ground of public confidence in the Government, will best ensure the beneficent ends of its institution." The preamble was a clear declaration that the amendments were needed, both to ensure personal liberties and to fulfill promises made to some states as a condition for ratifying the Constitution.

THE FIRST AMENDMENT

The first amendment covered significant ground in very few words: "Congress shall make no law respecting an establishment of religion, or prohibiting the free exercise thereof; or abridging the freedom of speech, or of the press; or the right of the people peaceably to assemble, and to petition the Government for a redress of grievances."

Although these rights and freedoms covered a wide range of circumstances, they were all individual liberties. They also shared a common heritage, as rights that had evolved in the states during their time as British colonies. Freedom of religion had surfaced as early as 1620, when the Pilgrims fled England searching for a place to worship as they pleased. (Unfortunately, while they had sought refuge in America to worship freely, they did not give other settlers in their colony the same opportunity. Dissent was not permitted.) The peaceful Quakers under William Penn had settled Pennsylvania in the 1680s and prospered in a fairly tolerant society. Meanwhile, the historical jockeying over the British throne between Catholics and Protestants (which finally led to the Catholic James II's abdication in 1688) had made colonial leaders sensitive to the dangers of mixing religion and politics.

A different sensitivity governed freedom of speech. In the American colonies of the 1700s, freedom of speech had become linked with criticism of the government. Any such criticism was a crime in England. But the ability to speak freely about the government without fear of retribution had gained increasing support in the colonies, especially as many Americans felt they had more and more to be critical about.

Freedom of speech was not just about talking in public. Expressing oneself without unfair restraints in print was equally valued. A famous legal case in 1735 had established the first important victory for freedom of the press in the colonies. In 1733, John Peter Zenger was the printer and publisher of the *New York Weekly Journal*, which often opposed the policies of the colonial governor, William Cosby. For a year, the paper printed scathing attacks on Cosby. At the time, criticizing the governor in print, whether fairly or not, was considered libelous and against the law. Finally, in 1734, Zenger was imprisoned. He was allowed, however, to continue to supervise the publication of the newspaper during the ten months he spent in jail awaiting trial.

John Peter Zenger apprenticed to William Bradford (with cane), before publishing his own paper, the *New York Weekly*. Zenger won his libel trial; this cartoon would have failed the accuracy test.

When Zenger's case went to court, he was defended by Andrew Hamilton, a well-known lawyer from Philadelphia. Hamilton had taken the case for free because the issue intrigued him. Rather than protest the innocence of his client (which would have been difficult since Zenger was guilty under the law), Hamilton challenged the rightness of the law that had allowed the governor to arrest Zenger in the first place. He spoke convincingly of this injustice, while at the same time demonstrating that Zenger's articles were all based on fact. Admittedly, the articles had damaged the governor's reputation—but only because they were true. Despite the existing laws, the jury found Zenger not guilty, sending a strong message that no government should be empowered to suppress the truth. In the future, with the precedent established for freedom of the press, political leaders would be more accountable to the public.

Assuring the right to assemble and to petition the government for changes represented a further attention to detail. The idea was to eliminate any loopholes or technicalities that would enable the government to control free speech. The right to speak freely wouldn't be of much use if public assemblies could be banned whenever the government chose. Then, too, the government had to remain accessible to petitions concerning any injustices that might take place. The hope was that clearly listing these provisions, leaving nothing to chance or goodwill, would make the government always accountable to the people it served.

THE SECOND AMENDMENT

At a time when wild animals and other dangers were a threat to anyone outside a major city, those who chose to own a gun did so without giving it much thought.

During the American Revolution, the Minutemen of Lexington and Concord acquired their name because they could, in times of need, grab their muskets at a minute's notice. Local militias continued to represent much of the American fighting force during the Revolution even after the Continental army was established.

So allowing people to bear arms was hardly controversial. And it was another way to create a check against a government-controlled army—should that army somehow be turned against the people. This had happened in the years before the Revolution, when the purpose and mission of the British troops stationed in America had changed rather abruptly. Their original purpose had been to defend the colonists against outside threats. But once disagreements arose with the mother country, the soldiers were used to impose Great Britain's will on an increasingly hostile population. To make sure that such an event was not repeated, the Second Amendment stated: "A well regulated Militia, being necessary to the security of a free State, the right of the people to keep and bear Arms, shall not be infringed."

"A well regulated Militia, being necessary to the security of a free State, the right of the people to keep and bear Arms, shall not be infringed."

—The Second Amendment

It was hoped that the ability of individual citizens to form armed militias would make any rogue generals or political leaders think twice before using the army to further their personal agendas. At the same time, the wording of the amendment seemed to allow anyone to bear arms, whether or not that person was a member of an organized civil military group.

THE THIRD AMENDMENT

Again, memories of the years before and during the Revolution were fresh in people's minds. The British military in America had done as it pleased during the early 1770s, taking over homes and buildings as resentment and opposition rose against colonial rule. Therefore, with respect to the United States' armed forces, the Third Amendment specified: "No Soldier shall, in time of peace be quartered in any house, without the consent of the Owner, nor in time of war, but in a manner to be prescribed by law."

Originally, the Federalists had objected that such protection against the quartering of troops was no longer needed, since the new government would truly serve its peoples' interests. But the population at large was not so trusting. And so this amendment promised further safeguards against potential abuses. With the phrase "but in a manner to be prescribed by law," Congress reserved the right to house soldiers in private homes during wartime if that was the best option available for maintaining the nation's defenses.

The Fourth Amendment protected people from being bullied, intimidated, or recklessly intruded upon in their private lives. It stated: "The right of the people to be secure in their persons, houses, papers, and effects, against unreasonable searches and seizures, shall not be violated, and no Warrants shall issue, but upon probable cause, supported by Oath or affirmation, and particularly describing the place to be searched, and the persons or things to be seized."

This meant that the government could not enter a house in search of criminal evidence just because it felt like doing so. Government officials would need a warrant issued by a judge in order to make searches and seize property. Moreover, search warrants would have to be specific. If the police were looking for stolen jewelry and came across stolen paintings, they would not be able to seize the paintings, because their warrant would have only covered jewelry. And even to search for the jewelry, they would have to present evidence to a judge showing that it was likely jewelry would be found. The government would not be allowed to engage in "fishing expeditions," hoping to find something incriminating in the homes of known suspects. Furthermore, anything obtained during an unlawful search, or during a lawful one if it was not the specific thing being searched for, would not be allowed as evidence in court.

Freedom of speech and the press were powerful rights as long as people remained at large in a society where they could express their views. But what if they were imprisoned, shut up from the outside world and unable to be heard? To protect against this possibility, the Fifth Amendment limited the power of the government to arbitrarily arrest and imprison people:

No person shall be held to answer for a capital, or otherwise infamous crime, unless on a presentment or indictment of a Grand Jury, except in cases arising in the land or naval forces, or in the Militia, when in actual service in time of War or public danger; nor shall any person be subject for the same offence to be twice put in jeopardy of life or limb; nor shall be compelled in any criminal case to be a witness against himself, nor be deprived of life, liberty, or property, without due process of law; nor shall private property be taken for public use, without just compensation.

A capital crime was one punishable by death. At the time, such crimes included murder and treason. An infamous crime, considered a little less severe—such as armed robbery or arson—was punishable by death or imprisonment. The Fifth Amendment guaranteed that no one would have to stand trial for such federal crimes unless he or she had been indicted by a grand jury. A grand jury's sole purpose was to decide whether there was enough evidence against the accused to hold a trial. Exceptions might be made in military cases when, in times of danger, national security might take precedence over individual rights.

The notion that a person cannot be put in double jeopardy, that is, put on trial for the same crime twice, was meant to protect suspects from being prosecuted prematurely for a crime. If a person could be tried for a crime only once, prosecutors would need to make sure their cases were strong before presenting them. Without this protection, citizens could be arrested again and again for the same crime, whenever new evidence or accusations surfaced. A person might, however, be tried a second time if a jury could not agree on a verdict, if a mistrial were to be declared, or if the accused person were to request a new trial.

The Fifth Amendment also guaranteed that a person could not be compelled to testify against himself. This protection was significant since it kept the government from prosecuting a person if the only evidence available would come from the testimony of that person himself.

The "due process of law" provision is one of the most important principles of the Constitution. It expresses the idea that a person's life, liberty, and property are not subject to the uncontrolled power of the government. It was designed to ensure that every

PROTECTION AGAINST SELF-INCRIMINATION

"Taking the Fifth" has become a popular phrase in books and movies as a way of referring to a defendant's right to invoke the Fifth Amendment's protections against self-incrimination. A defendant must claim this right at the beginning of any interrogation, either during an investigation or when called to testify at a trial. There is no option for claiming this defense once it has been waived by answering questions that are self-incriminating.

However, the amendment only serves as protection so long as there is a risk of prosecution to the defendant. Should the government offer immunity from prosecution in return for information or testimony, the amendment no longer can be used as a shield. This situation may arise when the government is interested in "bigger fish"—more notorious criminals whom the testimony of the arrested individual could help indict. If, after being guaranteed immunity, the accused person still refuses to testify, he or she can be jailed for contempt of court at the discretion of the judge in the case.

individual would receive fair treatment under the law. Without this protection, citizens opposing the government could be jailed on trumped-up charges and imprisoned for however long the government wished. Due process, like many of the other rights guaranteed in the Bill of Rights, could be traced back to the Magna Carta, which stated that the king might not imprison or harm a person "except by the lawful judgment of his peers or by the law of the land."

The last part of the amendment was a reminder that, while the government could commandeer private property for the larger good of society, it had to pay a fair price for whatever land or buildings it acquired. Again, a measure of protection and a degree of fairness were guaranteed to the individual under the law of the land.

THE SIXTH AMENDMENT

In keeping with the protection of personal freedoms and the limiting of government interference in the private life of an individual, the Sixth Amendment made sure that a person accused of a crime got a fair trial:

> In all criminal prosecutions, the accused shall enjoy the right to a speedy and public trial, by an impartial jury of the State and district wherein the crime shall have been committed, which district shall have been previously ascertained by law, and to be informed of the nature and cause

of the accusation; to be confronted with the witnesses against him; to have compulsory process for obtaining witnesses in his favor, and to have the Assistance of Counsel for his defense.

This amendment outlined step-by-step the rights that an arrested person was entitled to, including a timely trial by an unbiased jury, an explanation of the charges against him, an opportunity to call witnesses in his own defense, and an opportunity to confront hostile witnesses face-to-face. This last provision guaranteed that defendants had the opportunity to face and cross-examine their accusers. In doing so, they might be able to show that their accusers had lied or made a mistake.

In addition, the defendant's trial had to be held in public. A secret trial might be more vulnerable to abuses by the government. And if the defendant did not have the money to hire a lawyer, the government was required to provide one at no charge. Additionally, the trial would take place in the area where the crime had been committed so that the biases of a distant community would not be involved. However, selecting an impartial jury from the defendant's own community was and remains a difficult challenge.

THE SEVENTH AMENDMENT

The framers of the Constitution considered the right to trial by jury extremely important. While the Sixth

Amendment guaranteed jury trials in criminal cases, the Seventh provided for jury trials in civil cases, or monetary disputes between individuals or organizations, involving significant amounts of money: "In Suits at common law, where the value in controversy shall exceed twenty dollars, the right of trial by jury shall be preserved, and no fact tried by a jury, shall be otherwise re-examined in any Court of the United States, than according to the rules of the common law."

The twenty dollars cited as the minimum would translate to several hundred dollars today. Given that amount or more, the defendant in the case, the one who stood to lose the money, was entitled to a jury trial rather than one where a judge alone presided. Today, the amendment applies to nearly all civil cases. More important than the amount of money involved is the value placed on a person's right to a trial by jury.

The second part of this amendment defended the integrity of the jury system; a jury's factual decision could not be the subject of appeal. In most instances, only a matter of law or procedure could be appealed. If a jury resolved a case, that case could only be retried if the existing rules of common law allowed it. (Common law was defined as the body of laws already established from past cases.) It could not be tried again, for example, simply because the government was not satisfied with the verdict, if the verdict had followed the rules of law.

THE EIGHTH AMENDMENT

The Eighth Amendment sought to guarantee that bails, fines, and punishments would be fair and humane: "Excessive bail shall not be required, nor excessive fines imposed, nor cruel and unusual punishments inflicted."

Bail is money given to a court of law to allow the accused to remain out of jail until the time of his or her trial. The money is returned when the person appears for trial. If the accused flees, the bail is forfeited. The Eighth Amendment provided that bail could not be set so high that an ordinary person could not pay it, especially if the crime were a minor one. (For serious crimes such as murder, bail could be denied because the risk of flight would be too great.)

"Excessive bail shall not be required, nor excessive fines imposed, nor cruel and unusual punishments inflicted."

—The Eighth Amendment

If the accused was convicted, the amendment protected him or her from being fined excessively or punished in a cruel or unusual way. A murderer, for example, could no longer be put to death by such traditional procedures as being drawn and quartered or burned at the stake.

THE NINTH AMENDMENT

"The enumeration in the Constitution, of certain rights, shall not be construed to deny or disparage others retained by the people."

Some people feared that specifically listing some rights in the Bill of Rights would be interpreted to mean that other rights not mentioned were not protected. The Ninth Amendment was intended to prevent such a misinterpretation.

THE TENTH AMENDMENT

Although the Federalists had long argued that the Constitution limited the federal government to the roles specifically delegated to it, some people were still concerned that the states might be overpowered by the national government. The Tenth Amendment attempted to allay such fears: "The powers not delegated to the United States by the Constitution, nor prohibited by it to the States, are reserved to the States respectively, or to the people."

It was hoped that this amendment would finally put to rest the fear that the federal government would soon become a tyrannical beast oppressing the people far worse than Great Britain ever had. And it may have helped in that regard. However, the issue of states' rights versus the power of the federal government was not fully clarified. While the states had authority over such matters as marriage and divorce, the federal government, according to the Constitution, could make any laws "necessary and proper" to carry out its specific powers. It thus became difficult to determine exactly where the boundaries between the states and the national government lay.

With the ratification of the Bill of Rights, the country could now move forward and see whether the framework the Founding Fathers had established would actually function. There were several threats to its success. Across the Atlantic, the French Revolution, which shared many of the same ideals embodied in the Constitution, was erupting in violence and bloodshed. Clearly, it would be a mistake for Americans to take peace and prosperity for granted. Hovering like a dark shadow over the whole great experiment in democracy was the unresolved issue of slavery. Other threats, too, would arise from all sides of the political spectrum. There were no guarantees for the future, only a determined hope that things would work out in the end.

The first test of the Constitution came when John Adams, second president of the United States, signed the Alien and Sedition Acts into law.

Chapter Three

Constitutional Challenges

IF THE FOUNDING FATHERS BELIEVED that adding the Bill of Rights to the Constitution would settle most of the issues surrounding personal liberties once and for all, they were victims of wishful thinking. Certainly, the Bill of Rights cleared up some things, but in the years to come it would also prompt a great many debates.

In terms of long-term impact, not all ten amendments ended up with equal billing. The First Amendment was so full of important concerns that it would remain at the center of constitutional issues going forward. On the other hand, the Third Amendment, which prohibited quartering soldiers in private homes during peacetime, was pretty much ignored. It had been included because memories were still fresh of how the British had commandeered housing in the years leading up to the American Revolution. But as a country, the

United States never had the need to quarter troops in private homes, and so that issue faded away.

THE FIRST TEST

Enacting the Bill of Rights soon after the Constitution was ratified had been critical to getting the new country up and running. Once legalized, however, the amendments retreated into the background for a few years.

The first real test of the Constitution took place in 1798, during the presidency of John Adams. At the time, the United States was involved in an undeclared naval war with France. The chief supporters of the war were the Federalists, who controlled Congress. Adams, also a Federalist, signed four bills into law that were meant to silence opposition to the war. They were known as the Alien and Sedition Acts. Three of the laws made it difficult for foreigners to stay in the United States if the government wanted to deport them. But it was the fourth, the Sedition Act, that was the most noteworthy. Under its terms, publishing "false, scandalous, and malicious writing" against the government would now be a crime. The act took effect on July 14, 1798, and included an expiration date of March 3, 1801, when Adams's term as president would end. Although the act was meant to silence the voices of dissent, for many people it had the opposite effect. They objected to it as a violation of the free-speech provision of the First Amendment. Most prominent among the opponents was Vice President Thomas Jefferson, who was not a member of the Federalist Party and was generally sympathetic to France. Despite his opposition, the acts remained in force.

In the years to come, war, or the threat of war, would continue to serve as a justification for suspending freedom of speech. It was believed that voicing antigovernment sentiments during a military crisis was an unacceptable threat to national security. Protesters, even when they were not arrested, were often smeared with claims that they were traitors, or at least un-American, for not supporting the government's position.

Historically, the Supreme Court's record on freedom of speech has not been consistent, swinging one way or the other depending on the justices' perspectives at the time. In the last part of the twentieth century, public opinion generally backed giving protesters more latitude. However, in the months immediately following the attacks of September 11, 2001, tolerance for any kind of government criticism was muted at best.

THE SHIFTING BOUNDARIES OF CHURCH AND STATE

The first words written in the Bill of Rights concerned the delicate and potentially volatile subject of religion: "Congress shall make no law respecting an establishment of religion, or prohibiting the free exercise thereof."

In the long history of the world, many wars had been caused by religious differences. In an attempt to

CLEAR AND PRESENT DANGERS

One famous Supreme Court case in which the abridgment of freedom of speech was upheld occurred in 1919, during World War I. The circumstances in *Schenck v. United States* surrounded the distribution of a flyer opposing the draft. Freedom-of-speech advocates maintained that expressing an opinion contrary to the war effort should be protected under the Bill of Rights. Justice Oliver Wendell Holmes, writing the unanimous opinion of the Court, took a different view. The right to free speech could be curtailed when a "clear and present danger" to the country was involved. As an everyday example, Holmes mentioned that under no circumstances could the protection of free speech justify a person falsely shouting "Fire!" in a crowded theater.

In a later case, *Brandenburg v. Ohio*, the *Schenck* ruling was overturned. The Court decided that the distribution of flyers was too indirect a threat, even during a war, to warrant the suspension of the First Amendment's protection of freedom of speech.

Above: Justice Oliver Wendell Holmes decided that the First Amendment held no sway when the country was facing a "clear and present danger" in the form of war.

allow a person's faith to be his or her own private affair, there would be no established—or state—religion in the new republic, and all citizens would be free to practice their faith (or not) in their own way.

Religion was ingrained in the culture of America, as it was in most other places in the world. God was frequently invoked in official situations, whether in phrases such as "endowed by their Creator with certain unalienable rights," from the Declaration of Independence, or mottoes on money, such as "In God We Trust." The key difference in the United States was that the Constitution guaranteed that one could practice one's religion freely, with no coercion on the part of the government. Given the emotional intensity of the subject, however, religious conflicts have arisen from time to time.

SCHOOL PRAYER

Among the most well known of the conflicts over religious freedom concerned the subject of school prayer. In the nineteenth century, school prayer was commonly practiced across the country. Nobody seemed to mind, or at least those who might have minded were unwilling to make a fuss. But by the mid-twentieth century, serious objections about the constitutionality of school prayer arose. In 1962, in a landmark Supreme Court decision in the case of *Engel v. Vitale*, it was determined that state officials could not compose an official school prayer and require its recitation in public schools. The following year, in *Abington Township School District v. Schempp*, the Supreme Court declared that Bible reading in public schools was also unconstitutional.

These two decisions, plus others that followed in subsequent decades, created the current position that the First Amendment prohibits public schools from elevating one religion above another. Proponents of school prayer have continued to advocate for their position, but they have been unable to overturn these guidelines.

SALUTING THE FLAG

A different kind of friction had surfaced two decades before the school prayer debate. It concerned the saluting of the American flag in public schools. Within a span of four years, the Supreme Court took two different stands on whether it was constitutional to make saluting the flag and reciting the Pledge of Allegiance mandatory. The first case, *Minersville School District v. Gobitis*, began in 1935 in Pennsylvania. Two children, Lillian and William Gobitis, were expelled from school after following their parents' command not to participate in the daily saluting of the flag and recitation of the Pledge of Allegiance. The parents were Jehovah's Witnesses, and they considered saluting the flag to be akin to worshiping a graven image, something the Bible specifically forbids. The father sued the school system, insisting that his children's right to freedom of religion had been violated. The case reached the Supreme

William (*left*), Walter, and Lillian Gobitis are shown leaving the U.S. District Court in Philadelphia. The Gobitises cited the First Amendment as grounds for not saluting the flag.

Court in 1940 and the justices voted 8 to 1 in favor of the school system. Their explanation was that saluting the flag was a secular, or nonreligious, act and that a community could require compliance in the interest of fostering national loyalty.

Just three years later, a similar case, *West Virginia State Board of Education v. Barnette*, again involving Jehovah's Witnesses, reached the high court. Although only a short time had passed, the Court dramatically shifted its position. In a 6 to 3 decision, it decided that the West Virginia school system had violated both the students' freedom of speech and freedom of religion. Why the sudden change? Three new justices had joined the Court. One of them, Robert H. Jackson, wrote the majority opinion. Jackson explained that refusing to salute the flag or recite the pledge might

> "If there is any fixed star in our constitutional constellation, it is that no official, high or petty, can prescribe what shall be orthodox in politics, nationalism, religion, or other matters of opinion or force citizens to confess by word or act their faith therein."
>
> —Supreme Court Justice Robert H. Jackson

be a form of political protest or might reflect a conscientious decision on the part of a person of devout religious belief. In either case, this symbolic expression was protected by the First Amendment. "If there is any fixed star in our constitutional constellation," he wrote, "it is that no official, high or petty, can prescribe what shall be orthodox in politics, nationalism, religion, or other matters of opinion or force citizens to confess by word or act their faith therein."

Jackson underscored the point as plainly as he could: "Freedom is not limited to things that do not matter much. That would be a mere shadow of freedom. The test of its substance is the right to differ as to things that touch the heart of the existing order."

THE RIGHT TO BEAR ARMS

For many years, the Second Amendment's protection of a citizen's right to bear arms drew little attention from the public. One reason was that the United States did not have a large standing army, and average citizens might well expect to be called on to defend their country. At such times, those citizens would naturally want to be prepared. Moreover, the Uniform Militia Act of 1792 required every "free able-bodied white male citizen" to enlist in a local militia under the supervision of the state. These men had to supply their own guns and ammunition, as well as report for training twice a year.

So the idea of owning a gun was pretty much taken for granted. Even outside the military, people living on the frontier used their guns for hunting and defense. The right to bear arms was no more noteworthy than growing up in a log cabin or learning to read by the light of a hearth fire. Lots of people did all three.

As the need to hunt for the family's daily dinner lessened, bearing arms became more controversial. Attention was drawn to the very specific wording of the amendment. The opening phrase read, "A well regulated Militia, being necessary to the security of a free State." Was that meant to modify the main phrase, "the right of the people to keep and bear Arms shall not be infringed"? If so, then bearing arms would be tied to participating in a militia. But another interpretation insisted that the two phrases were not inextricably bound. According to this logic, a militia was simply one example of why protecting the right to bear arms was a good idea. And neither interpretation conclusively explained whether any and all arms—machine guns as well as hunting rifles, for example—should be covered by the amendment. As with other rights issues such as freedom of speech and religion, the Supreme Court initially left the states to decide this matter for themselves.

Once the Bill of Rights gained precedence over state laws, further interpretation was necessary. Over the years, strong opinions have been aired on both sides. Law enforcement agencies, for example, have favored placing restrictions on weapons or ammunition (such as armor-piercing bullets) that put their officers at particular risk. Opposing this view are organizations such as the National Rifle Association, which insist that any limitations run counter to the spirit and wording of the amendment itself.

Most recently, in a 2008 ruling in the case of *District of Columbia v. Heller,* the Supreme Court stated that the Second Amendment protects a person's right to possess a firearm regardless of whether or not that person participates in any kind of militia. Although this seemed to accept a broad interpretation of the amendment, the Court also made it clear that its ruling was not meant to overturn existing bans on gun ownership by felons or the mentally ill. The ruling also was not meant to cast doubt on the banning of firearms from places such as schools and government buildings.

Richard Heller signed the placards of supporters after the Supreme Court ruled in his favor on the right to bear arms under the Second Amendment.

Legal cases such as this will no doubt continue to draw the Supreme Court's attention, perhaps keeping the Second Amendment the most unsettled of any provision in the Bill of Rights.

THE SEARCH GOES ON

As with many other provisions in the Bill of Rights, the motivation behind the Fourth Amendment—which prohibits unlawful searches and seizures—had its roots in the actions of the British forces in colonial America. In the years before the American Revolution, government officials could search homes and businesses whenever they wanted. They did not need evidence to support their actions. A vague rumor, a whisper of suspicion—these were more than enough to justify an investigation. Sometimes, too, these actions were politically motivated. For example, ransacking the home of a rabble-rouser for evidence of a "crime" could discourage that person from continuing to cause trouble for the ruling authorities.

The Fourth Amendment curtailed such tactics—at least to the extent that the Founding Fathers could predict them. Unreasonable searches originally referred to papers, books, or household belongings, all of which existed in the late 1700s. Of course, times changed, not only in terms of viewpoints and philosophies but also in terms of technology. Nobody, for example, foresaw the invention of the telephone, which led to a new kind of potential "search" in the form of wiretapping.

In *Olmstead v. United States*, a case that came before the Supreme Court in 1928, a man named Roy Olmstead protested that his conviction on charges of bootlegging (illegally transporting and selling alcohol), gained largely on evidence gath-

Left: Elise and Roy Olmstead in a Seattle photo, 1925. *Opposite page*: Supreme Court Justice Louis Brandeis wrote a stinging dissent in the *Olmstead* case.

ered by the government's tapping of his phone, represented an unlawful search since the wiretapping was done without a warrant. The Court voted 5 to 4 against his contention, because the tap had not physically violated his home. In a stinging dissent, Justice Louis D. Brandeis cited the Fourth and Fifth Amendments' clear intent to establish a person's right to privacy. This, he firmly believed, meant "the right to be left alone—the most comprehensive of rights and the right most valued by civilized men. To protect that right, every unjustifiable intrusion by the Government upon the privacy of the individual, whatever the means employed, must be deemed a violation of the Fourth Amendment."

For almost forty years, Brandeis's words stood as an unheeded warning against privacy intrusions. Then, in 1967, in *Katz v. United States*, the Supreme Court finally ruled that wiretapping without a warrant was indeed unconstitutional and that monitoring phone conversations

"... the right to be left alone—the most comprehensive of rights and the right most valued by civilized men. To protect that right, every unjustifiable intrusion by the Government upon the privacy of the individual ... must be deemed a violation of the Fourth Amendment."

—Supreme Court Justice Louis D. Brandeis

must be governed like any other search. Since that time, many other technological advances, such as high-tech listening devices and the ability to track Internet activity, have become common. The Supreme Court now maintains that the Fourth Amendment provides protection again any unwarranted searches, electronic or otherwise.

ARRESTING DEVELOPMENTS

When the prohibition against self-incrimination was included in the Fifth Amendment, it was considered fairly straightforward. The principle was simple enough—a person accused of a crime should not be forced to testify against himself. However, the Founding Fathers lived in a simpler society, where almost everyone spoke English and shared a similar heritage.

By the mid-twentieth century, the country had experienced a great influx of immigrants from many different countries. Their ability to speak and understand English might be limited, and they likely would not be familiar with American culture. Under these circumstances, it was not fair to assume that individuals who were arrested would be aware of their Fifth Amendment rights, especially if they came from countries where such rights did not exist.

In 1966, the case of *Miranda v. Arizona* came before the Supreme Court. Ernesto Miranda was arrested for robbery and rape after a crime victim identified him. The arresting officers, however, did not inform him of his Fifth Amendment right against self-incrimination or of his Sixth Amendment right to the assistance of an attorney during questioning. Miranda confessed to the crime, and his confession became a key element in his subsequent conviction. However, he appealed his case until the Supreme Court agreed to hear it.

Miranda's lawyer argued before the Court that Miranda's confession should have been excluded from his trial because he had not been informed of his rights at the time of his arrest. The Court agreed and ruled, with Chief Justice Earl Warren writing the majority opinion, that Miranda's confession was inadmissible. His conviction, therefore, was overturned. The Court then established guidelines for arresting officers to follow from that time forward.

Immediately upon being taken into custody, a suspect must be told his rights. The wording may vary a little from state to state, but the statement has become well known through its appearance in various fictional crime dramas: "You have the right to remain silent. Anything you say can and will be used against you in a court of law. You have the right to an attorney present during questioning. If you cannot afford an attorney, one will be appointed for you." Supreme Court decisions in 2010 now make it necessary for the suspect to say he or she wants to remain silent.

An arrested person's rights extend well beyond the moment of the arrest itself. The Sixth Amendment also covered a defendant's right to a speedy trial. A speedy trial was and remains more than simply a convenience or mark of respect for the accused. The defendant, after all, is presumed innocent until proven guilty. If a speedy trial does not take place, the Supreme Court has ruled that the defendant should be set free. No specific timetable, though, has been established to assess whether a case is staying on schedule. Gathering evidence and collecting testimony can take varying amounts of time depending on, for example, the location of witnesses or the nature of the evidence being examined. (Examining fingerprints is easier than sifting through the pulverized remains of an explosion.)

HOW CRUEL AND UNUSUAL CAN A PUNISHMENT BE?

The Founding Fathers' objection to "cruel and unusual punishments" was based on humane principles. In medieval times, punishment by death had often deliberately included torture in order to prolong the condemned prisoner's pain. The Eighth Amendment, which prohibited such practices, reflected changing eighteenth-century views. If someone was condemned to die, the death itself was now considered enough of a penalty. Anything more was deemed excessive.

The definition of "excessive," however, left some wiggle room. In the nineteenth century, death by hanging was still a public spectacle. Apparently, it was not considered cruel or unusual for the victim's last moments to serve as entertainment for anyone who chose to watch. In more recent times, executions have become closed to the general public. The form of execution, though, still varies. Some states favor lethal injection or a gas chamber. Others use the electric chair.

The death penalty itself has become very controversial. Many people believe that it is morally wrong for the government to put an individual to death. They

Though we now consider it barbaric, hanging people from the gallows was still common in the 1800s, as in this Delaware hanging post, circa 1834.

believe that no one has the right to take another's life. While other countries, such as the United Kingdom, have outlawed the death penalty, the United States still considers the punishment constitutional. The death penalty continues to be the law of the land although fewer and fewer executions are performed each year.

BOUNDARIES AND LIMITS

One of the biggest challenges to the Bill of Rights has focused on the extent of its jurisdiction. James Madison had sought to include an amendment that would ensure that the new rights applied to state as well as federal jurisdictions. But his effort failed. Instead, the Ninth and Tenth Amendments explained that rights not specifically granted to the federal government in the Constitution were reserved to the people or the states.

Issues naturally arose. In 1833, the Supreme Court heard the case of *Barron v. Mayor and City Council of Baltimore*. John Barron, who owned a wharf in the Baltimore harbor, had sued the local government for damages his property had received when the city diverted a nearby stream. The resulting buildup of silt had made his wharf largely unusable. Under the Fifth Amendment, specifically the clause stating that "private property" could not be "taken for public use, without just compensation," Barron claimed that he was entitled to receive fair payment for his loss. But the Supreme Court ruled that the Fifth Amendment (and all others) applied only to actions taken by the federal government. And so it didn't apply in this case.

Perhaps inevitably, some of the greatest threats to the nation have come through a test of how much power a state actually retains. The Civil War, for example, was fought partly over the claim by the Southern states that they had the legal right to secede from a union that no longer met their needs. President Abraham Lincoln disagreed. The war itself settled the matter. As the years passed, the views of the people changed, and with them changed the decisions of the Supreme Court. Particularly in the case of civil rights, federal jurisdiction has come to supersede that of the states.

WE SHOULD ALWAYS REMEMBER THAT it was the promise of the Bill of Rights, and the confidence people had in the ideals it would represent, that enabled the backers of the Constitution to get the support they needed. Without that promise, the Constitution would not have been ratified and the United States as we know it would not exist today.

Clearly, the Bill of Rights was an absolutely crucial part of our nation's foundation. William Gladstone, the nineteenth-century British prime minister, described the U.S. Constitution as "the most remarkable work known to me in modern times to have been produced by the human intellect, at a single stroke (so to speak) in its application to political affairs." And maybe it was. But the Constitution was designed to articulate the workings of a republican form of government. It was the brains of the operation. The heart of that government, its ideals, were embodied in the document's first ten amendments, the Bill of Rights.

For many years after the Constitution took effect, those rights were not applied equally across the country. Individual states still had jurisdiction over personal freedoms in their domains. And some of those states, and the people in charge of them, did not hesitate to ignore individual rights when it suited their purpose. Slaves in particular had little protection. They were considered a valuable form of property.

The Civil War brought an end to slavery, although the laws that sprang up in several of the states after the war still allowed many inequities to flourish. Only once the Supreme Court began to insist that the Bill of Rights superseded any state laws did the beginnings of consistent freedoms emerge.

The Constitution and the Bill of Rights continue to evolve today. The debate remains about what the right to bear arms truly means and where the line should be drawn in issues surrounding religion and the state. Resolving such questions is a difficult task, at least partly because there may not be any perfect solution. And even reaching the right solution for one generation may prove to be insufficient for those to come.

Still, the Bill of Rights remains a strong anchor for the nation. No matter what point of the political spectrum has the upper hand at the moment, the first ten amendments represent a guide for how an ethical and fair society should conduct itself—both now and in the future.

The Bill of Rights

FROM THE U.S. NATIONAL ARCHIVES &
RECORDS ADMINISTRATION

THE PREAMBLE

Congress OF THE *United States begun and held at the City of New-York, on Wednesday the fourth of March, one thousand seven hundred and eighty nine.*

THE Conventions of a number of the States, having at the time of their adopting the Constitution, expressed a desire, in order to prevent misconstruction or abuse of its powers, that further declaratory and restrictive clauses should be added: And as extending the ground of public confidence in the Government, will best ensure the beneficent ends of its institution.

RESOLVED by the Senate and House of Representatives of the United States of America, in Congress assembled, two thirds of both Houses concurring, that the following Articles be proposed to the Legislatures of the several States, as amendments to the Constitution of the United States, all, or any of which Articles, when ratified by three fourths of the said Legislatures, to be valid to all intents and purposes, as part of the said Constitution; viz.

ARTICLES in addition to, and Amendment of the Constitution of the United States of America, proposed by Congress, and ratified by the Legislatures of the several States, pursuant to the fifth Article of the original Constitution.

AMENDMENT I

Congress shall make no law respecting an establishment of religion, or prohibiting the free exercise thereof; or abridging the freedom of speech, or of the press; or the right of the people peaceably to assemble, and to petition the Government for a redress of grievances.

AMENDMENT II

A well regulated Militia, being necessary to the security of a free State, the right of the people to keep and bear Arms, shall not be infringed.

AMENDMENT III

No Soldier shall, in time of peace be quartered in any house, without the consent of the Owner, nor in time of war, but in a manner to be prescribed by law.

AMENDMENT IV

The right of the people to be secure in their persons, houses, papers, and effects, against unreasonable searches and seizures, shall not be violated, and no Warrants shall issue, but upon probable cause, supported by Oath or affirmation, and particularly describing the place to be searched, and the persons or things to be seized.

AMENDMENT V

No person shall be held to answer for a capital, or otherwise infamous crime, unless on a presentment or indictment of a Grand Jury, except in cases arising in the land or naval forces, or in the Militia, when in actual service in time of War or public danger; nor shall any person be subject for the same offence to be twice put in jeopardy of life or limb; nor shall be compelled in any criminal case to be a witness against himself, nor be deprived of life, liberty, or property, without due process of law; nor shall private property be taken for public use, without just compensation.

AMENDMENT VI

In all criminal prosecutions, the accused shall enjoy the right to a speedy and public trial, by an impartial jury of the State and district wherein the crime shall have been committed, which district shall have been previously ascertained by law, and to be informed of the nature and cause of the accusation; to be confronted with the witnesses against him; to have compulsory process for obtaining witnesses in his favor, and to have the Assistance of Counsel for his defence.

AMENDMENT VII

In Suits at common law, where the value in controversy shall exceed twenty dollars, the right of trial by jury shall be preserved, and no fact tried by a jury, shall be otherwise re-examined in any Court of the United States, than according to the rules of the common law.

AMENDMENT VIII

Excessive bail shall not be required, nor excessive fines imposed, nor cruel and unusual punishments inflicted.

AMENDMENT IX

The enumeration in the Constitution, of certain rights, shall not be construed to deny or disparage others retained by the people.

AMENDMENT X

The powers not delegated to the United States by the Constitution, nor prohibited by it to the States, are reserved to the States respectively, or to the people.

NOTES

PROMISES TO KEEP

p. 7, "unalienable rights . . .": Robert Maynard
Hutchins, ed. in chief, *Great Books of the Western
World* (Chicago: Encyclopaedia Britannica, 1952),
43:1.

p. 7, "Is it to be supposed . . .": Vine Deloria Jr. and
David E. Wilkins, *Tribes, Treaties and Constitutional
Tribulations* (Austin, TX: University of Texas Press,
1999), 22.

CHAPTER ONE: A QUESTION OF RIGHTS

p. 14, "that in all . . .": http://www.constitution.org/bcp/
virg_dor.htm

p. 18, "sooner chop off . . .": Leonard W. Levy, *Origins of
the Bill of Rights* (New Haven, CT: Yale University
Press, 1999), 14.

p. 20, "I think liberty . . .": Richard Labunski, *James
Madison and the Struggle for the Bill of Rights* (New
York: Oxford University Press, 2006), 30.

p. 23, "for putting . . .": http://www.archives.gov/
exhibits/charters/constitution_history.html

p. 24, "It cannot be a secret . . .": Ibid., 19–20.

CHAPTER TWO: "THE GREAT RIGHTS OF MANKIND"

p. 30, "The Conventions of a . . .": http://www.archives.
gov/exhibits/charters/bill_of_rights_transcript.html

p. 30, "Congress shall make . . .": Ibid.

p. 34, "A well regulated . . .": Ibid.

p. 35, "No Soldier shall . . .": Ibid.

p. 36, "The right of the people . . .": Ibid.

p. 37, "No person shall be held . . .": Ibid.

p. 40, "except by the lawful . . .": Paul Finkleman, *The Encyclopedia of American Civil Liberties*, vol. 1, *A-F* (New York: Routledge, 2006), 456.

p. 40, "In all criminal prosecutions . . .": http://www. archives.gov/exhibits/charters/bill_of_rights_ transcript.html

p. 42, "In Suits at . . .": Ibid.

p. 43, "Excessive bail . . .": Ibid.

p. 43, "The enumeration in the . . .": Ibid.

p. 44, "The powers not delegated . . .": Ibid.

p. 44, "necessary and proper . . .": Henry Hyde, presenter, *The Constitution of the United States* (Washington, DC: U.S. Government Printing Office, 2000), 5.

CHAPTER THREE: CONSTITUTIONAL CHALLENGES

p. 48, "false, scandalous . . .": http://www.constitution. org/rf/sedition_1798.htm

p. 49, "Congress shall make . . .": Henry Hyde, presenter, *The Constitution of the United States* (Washington, DC: U.S. Government Printing Office, 2000), 13.

p. 51, "endowed by their . . .": Robert Maynard Hutchins,

ed. in chief, *Great Books of the Western World* (Chicago: Encyclopaedia Britannica, 1952), 43:1.

p. 54, "If there is . . .": http://law.jrank.org/pages/6931/Flag-Salute-Cases.html

p. 54, "Freedom is not . . .": Edmund Lindop, *The Bill of Rights and Landmark Cases* (New York: Franklin Watts, 1989), 41.

p. 55, "free able-bodied . . .": http://www.constitution.org/mil/mil_act_1792.htm

p. 55, "A well regulated . . .": Henry Hyde, presenter, *The Constitution of the United States* (Washington, DC: U.S. Government Printing Office, 2000), 13.

p. 59, "the right to be . . .": Russell Freedman, *In Defense of Liberty: The Story of America's Bill of Rights* (New York: Holiday House, 2003), 90–91.

p. 61, "You have the right . . .": Rich Smith, *Fifth Amendment: The Right to Fairness* (Edina, MN: ABDO Publishing, 2008), 12.

p. 62, "cruel and unusual . . .": http://www.archives.gov/exhibits/charters/bill_of_rights_transcript.html

p. 64, "private property . . .": Ibid.

CONCLUSION

p. 65, "the most remarkable . . .": John Bartlett, *Bartlett's Familiar Quotations*, 16th ed., edited by Justin Kaplan (Boston: Little, Brown and Company, 1992), 447.

All Internet sites were accurate and accessible as of February 15, 2011.

BOOKS

Freedman, Russell. *In Defense of Liberty: The Story of America's Bill of Rights.* New York: Holiday House, 2003.

Krull, Kathleen. *A Kids' Guide to America's Bill of Rights.* New York: Avon Books, 1999.

Levy, Leonard W. *Origins of the Bill of Rights.* New Haven, CT: Yale University Press, 1999.

Meltzer, Milton. *The Bill of Rights: How We Got It and What It Means.* New York: Thomas Y. Crowell, 1990.

WEBSITES

The Charters of Freedom

www.archives.gov/exhibits/charters/bill_of_rights.html
The U.S. Government Archives feature a close-up look at the Bill of Rights and descriptions of surrounding issues and events.

First Amendment Center

www.firstamendmentschools.org
This site provides a variety of information about the First Amendment and its place in society.

Revolutionary War and Beyond
www.revolutionary-war-and-beyond.com/fifth-
amendment-court-cases-due-process-clause.html
This site examines the many important court cases
influenced by the Fifth Amendment and provides
links to information about the other amendments
in the Bill of Rights.

All Internet sites were accurate and accessible as of February 15, 2011.

Cogan, Neil H., ed. *The Complete Bill of Rights: The Drafts, Debates, Sources, & Origins.* New York: Oxford University Press, 1997.

Freedman, Russell. *In Defense of Liberty: The Story of America's Bill of Rights.* New York: Holiday House, 2003.

Labunski, Richard. *James Madison and the Struggle for the Bill of Rights.* New York: Oxford University Press, 2006.

Lindop, Edmund. *The Bill of Rights and Landmark Cases.* New York: Franklin Watts, 1989.

Meltzer, Milton. *The Bill of Rights: How We Got It and What It Means.* New York: Thomas Y. Crowell, 1990.

ABOUT THE AUTHOR

STEPHEN KRENSKY is the author of more than one hundred fiction and nonfiction books for children, including many about American history. He has written chapter-book biographies of Barack Obama, Benjamin Franklin, and George Washington as well as shorter works on the Salem witch trials, Paul Revere, John Adams, the California gold rush, George Washington Carver, Annie Oakley, and the Wright Brothers.